WHAT TRAINING MY DOG TAUGHT ME ABOUT LEADERSHIP

52 Practical Lessons in Patience, Clarity, and Leading with Confidence

MARTY PEARSON

QUANTUM SHIFT
PUBLISHING
Port St. Lucie, Florida

Cover and interior design by QuantumShiftMedia.com

Photographs provided courtesy of Critter Pics Pet Photography, critterpics.net, info@critterpics.net.

Paperback 978-1-955533-46-1
Hardback 978-1-955533-47-8
eBook 978-1-955533-48-5

Library of Congress Control Number: pending

Printed in the United States of America

QUANTUM SHIFT
PUBLISHING

Port St. Lucie, Florida

What Training My Dog Taught Me About Leadership

Acknowledgments

A huge thank-you to my wonderfully chaotic dog, Beanie, without whom this book would never have been created.

Beanie, your selective hearing, dramatic sighs, squirrel-hunting, and uncanny ability to ignore a command until a treat is involved have taught me more about leadership than any workshop ever could.

Thank you for reminding me that patience is a virtue, consistency is non-negotiable, and sometimes the best thing a leader can do is laugh, take a breath, and try again tomorrow.

This book is dedicated to you,
my furry, four-legged friend.

Introduction

If you have ever trained a dog, you know it takes patience, consistency, and a good sense of humor. In my own efforts to train my dog over the last few years, I discovered something surprising: the very principles that make training successful are the same ones that make leadership successful.

Clear communication. Trust. Encouragement. Boundaries. Kindness. Patience.

Whether you are teaching a puppy to sit or guiding a team through a project, the techniques are remarkably similar.

This book grew out of that realization. Inside, you will find 52 leadership lessons I learned while training my dog. Each one includes a tip from training, a leadership takeaway, and a reflection question. My hope is that you won't just read these lessons, but you will apply them to your work, your business, and your life.

How To Use This Book

One Lesson A Week: The book is designed to be read one page (one lesson) per week. That gives you a full year of leadership growth, bite-sized and practical.

Reflect & Journal: At the end of each lesson, you'll find a reflection question. Use it as a journal prompt, a team discussion starter, or simply something to ponder as you lead that week.

Apply in Real Life: These lessons only work if you put them into practice. Just as a dog doesn't learn "sit" by watching, your leadership won't grow without action. Choose one small way each week to apply the principle.

Come Back Often: Like dog training, leadership isn't one-and-done. You'll find new insights each time you revisit these lessons.

Reward the Behavior You Want

Dog Training Insight: When teaching a dog to sit, you don't give the treat when they jump. You give it when they sit. The timing matters.

Leadership Lesson: The same is true with people. Recognize and reward the behaviors you want repeated. If you only notice mistakes, that's what your team remembers. A well-timed "good job" is often more powerful than a corrective meeting.

Reflection: What specific behaviors do I want to see more of on my team, and how can I reinforce them this week?

Consistency Builds Trust

Dog Training Insight: If you let the dog on the couch one day and scold them the next, they don't know what to expect. Inconsistency creates anxiety.

Leadership Lesson: Employees feel the same way. A consistent leader sets clear boundaries and expectations and sticks to them. Consistency builds trust, while inconsistency builds frustration.

Reflection: Where might I be inconsistent in my leadership, and how can I correct that?

Clear Commands Work Best

Dog Training Insight: Dogs respond better to "sit" than to a long sentence like "Why don't you go ahead and sit down now?" Simplicity wins.

Leadership Lesson: At work, clarity is kindness. People need straightforward instructions, not a rambling explanation. The clearer the message, the fewer mistakes, and the stronger the results.

Reflection: What's one instruction or goal I could simplify today to reduce confusion?

Tone of Voice Matters

Dog Training Insight: Dogs respond as much to the tone of "good boy!" as to the words. Encouragement carries power.

Leadership Lesson: People also hear your tone before your words. A supportive, confident tone motivates, while a harsh or dismissive tone discourages, even if the message is the same.

Reflection: How does my tone (in person, email, meetings) impact my team's response?

Be Present

Dog Training Insight: Training works best when you're fully engaged, not scrolling your phone.

Leadership Lesson: Teams notice when leaders are distracted. Being fully present in a conversation shows respect and strengthens connection.

Reflection: In what situations do I get most distracted as a leader, and how can I show up more fully?

Body Language Speaks Volumes

Dog Training Insight: A stiff posture tells a dog something very different than relaxed shoulders. They watch more than they listen.

Leadership Lesson: Teams read your body language too. Leaders communicate confidence, openness, or stress without saying a word.

Reflection: What does my nonverbal communication say when I'm stressed or rushed?

Set Realistic Expectations

Dog Training Insight: You can't expect a puppy to heel like a champion on day one. Start with the basics.

Leadership Lesson: Leaders need to match expectations to skill level. Asking too much too soon sets people up for failure.

Reflection: Am I asking too much, too soon from anyone on my team right now?

Trust Takes Time

Dog Training Insight: A rescue dog won't trust you instantly. Consistent care earns it slowly.

Leadership Lesson: New employees don't automatically trust leadership. Reliability, honesty, and follow-through build confidence over time.

Reflection: Where do I need to invest more time to build trust with my team?

Stay Positive

Dog Training Insight: Positive reinforcement leads to better learning than constant correction. Dogs thrive on encouragement.

Leadership Lesson: People are the same. When leaders focus on strengths and wins, performance improves far faster than under criticism alone.

Reflection: How can I intentionally highlight the positive this week?

Boundaries Create Freedom

Dog Training Insight: A fenced yard allows a dog to run free without danger. Boundaries aren't punishment, they're protection.

Leadership Lesson: Employees thrive with clear expectations. Rules and guardrails don't limit, they empower people to work confidently without fear of stepping into trouble.

Reflection: Do my team members know the clear "rules of the game"?

Be the Pack Leader, Not the Bully

Dog Training Insight: Dogs respect calm authority, not harsh dominance. Leadership is about guidance, not intimidation.

Leadership Lesson: Employees don't follow bullies, they follow leaders they respect. Authority without care erodes trust; authority with respect builds loyalty.

Reflection: Do my people follow me out of respect, or fear? How do I know?

Meet Them Where They Are

Dog Training Insight: You don't train a shy rescue the same way you train an eager puppy. The starting point matters.

Leadership Lesson: Leaders should meet employees where they are, considering background, experience, and confidence. Growth starts from their current position, not your ideal.

Reflection: How well do I adapt to my team members' starting points and backgrounds?

Build Trust Through Small Promises

Dog Training Insight: When you always come back after leaving for a while, they learn you can be trusted.

Leadership Lesson: Trust in leadership is built by keeping small commitments, showing up on time, following through on promises, and proving reliability day after day.

Reflection: What's one small promise I can make, and keep this week to reinforce trust?

Patience Pays Off

Dog Training Insight: Teaching a puppy "stay" requires repetition and patience. Rushing only leads to confusion.

Leadership Lesson: Growth, whether in skills or confidence, takes time. As a leader, patience allows others the space to learn and succeed at their own pace. Pressure to "get it right now" usually backfires.

Reflection: Where do I need to slow down and give others more time to grow?

Practice Daily, Not Just Occasionally

Dog Training Insight: A dog won't master recall if you only practice once a month. Daily practice builds reliability.

Leadership Lesson: Leadership is no different. Don't save feedback, coaching, or recognition for the annual review. Make it a daily habit. Consistent small actions shape lasting results.

Reflection: What leadership habit should I commit to practicing daily?

Start Simple Before Going Complex

Dog Training Insight: You don't begin with obstacle courses, you start with "sit" and "stay." The foundation makes the advanced possible.

Leadership Lesson: At work, don't overwhelm people with complexity before they've mastered the basics. Build confidence step by step, then layer on more responsibility.

Reflection: *Where am I over complicating things instead of simplifying?*

Correct in the Moment

Dog Training Insight: A dog only connects the correction to the action if it happens immediately. Delays weaken the lesson.

Leadership Lesson: Feedback is most effective when it's timely. Correcting a mistake weeks later just breeds confusion. Leaders should act in the moment while the behavior is fresh.

Reflection: Do I hold onto feedback too long instead of giving it in real time?

Don't Punish Mistakes—Redirect

Dog Training Insight: Instead of scolding for chewing a shoe, give the dog a toy. Redirecting teaches them what to do, not just what not to do.

Leadership Lesson: Employees need constructive redirection more than criticism. Instead of dwelling on the error, show them the better way forward.

Reflection: How can I turn a mistake into a teachable moment this week?

Prepare Before You Train

Dog Training Insight: A good trainer sets the stage before starting, treats ready, distractions minimized, leash in hand. Preparation makes success easier.

Leadership Lesson: Leaders often dive into meetings or conversations without preparation, which leads to confusion and wasted time. Taking a few minutes to clarify your goal and gather resources creates a more productive outcome.

Reflection: How can I prepare more intentionally before my next meeting, conversation, or project?

Celebrate Small Wins

Dog Training Insight: A puppy learning "down" may only lower halfway at first, but that progress is worth rewarding.

Leadership Lesson: In business, celebrate incremental success. Recognizing small wins fuels momentum toward bigger goals.

Reflection: What small win can I celebrate with my team today?

Repetition Builds Mastery

Dog Training Insight: A dog doesn't "know" a command after one success, it takes practice to make it reliable.

Leadership Lesson: Skills at work also require repeated practice. One training session doesn't create mastery; consistency does.

Reflection: What skill or behavior do I need to reinforce more consistently?

End on a High Note

Dog Training Insight: Trainers finish with a trick the dog already knows. Success keeps the dog eager for next time.

Leadership Lesson: End meetings or coaching sessions with positivity. Leave people motivated to return, not drained.

Reflection: Do my meetings and conversations leave people motivated or drained?

Different Rewards Motivate Different Dogs

Dog Training Insight: Some love food, others toys, others praise. The motivator is unique.

Leadership Lesson: Employees are motivated by different things recognition, growth, flexibility, pay. A one-size-fits-all approach misses the mark.

Reflection: Do I know what motivates each team member? If not, how can I find out?

Routine Builds Confidence

Dog Training Insight: Walking the same route helps a nervous dog build comfort. Familiarity builds trust.

Leadership Lesson: Consistent systems and rituals help teams feel grounded. Predictability gives confidence to explore new challenges.

Reflection: What regular rhythms or routines could I introduce to create stability?

Transitions Matter

Dog Training Insight: Moving a dog from playtime to training or from indoors to outdoors requires a smooth transition. Abrupt changes create resistance.

Leadership Lesson: Leaders often underestimate the power of transitions, such as starting a meeting, shifting priorities, or changing strategies. How you guide people into and through transitions determines whether they resist or adapt.

Reflection: What transition am I leading my team through right now, and how can I make it smoother?

Adjust for the Breed

Dog Training Insight: A herding dog learns and works differently than a lapdog. Their instincts shape how they respond.

Leadership Lesson: Every employee brings natural strengths and tendencies. The best leaders lean into those differences instead of fighting them.

Reflection: How well am I aligning work to the natural strengths of my team members?

Keep Sessions Fun

Dog Training Insight: When training feels like play, dogs learn faster.

Leadership Lesson: Work doesn't always need to be heavy. Laughter, creativity, and joy fuel engagement and innovation.

Reflection: What's one way I could add more enjoyment or creativity into work this week?

Short Sessions Beat Marathons

Dog Training Insight: Ten minutes of focused training is more effective than an hour-long grind.

Leadership Lesson: People learn best in short, intentional bursts. Long meetings and drawn-out trainings reduce retention and motivation.

Reflection: Am I overwhelming my team with too much at once?

Over Training Backfires

Dog Training Insight: Push too long and the dog zones out or resists.

Leadership Lesson: Burnout happens when leaders push without rest. People perform best with balance, not endless demands.

Reflection: Where might I be pushing too hard instead of allowing rest?

Be Patient With New Environments

Dog Training Insight: A dog who knows a trick indoors may freeze outside with distractions. Patience is key.

Leadership Lesson: Employees need time to adjust when facing new roles, teams, or settings. Don't assume they'll perform instantly.

Reflection: Who on my team is adjusting to a new role or situation and how can I support them?

Watch for Cues

Dog Training Insight: A tucked tail, perked ears, or a yawn tells you volumes. Dogs communicate in signals.

Leadership Lesson: Employees also send subtle cues tone of voice, body language, silence. Leaders who notice can respond with empathy before issues escalate.

Reflection: What subtle signals am I noticing or missing from my team?

Don't Compare

Dog Training Insight: Expecting one dog to train at another's pace leads to frustration. Every learner is different.

Leadership Lesson: Teams are made of individuals with unique strengths and learning curves. Comparisons demotivate; personalized support empowers.

Reflection: Am I unfairly comparing one person's progress to another's?

Flexibility Matters

Dog Training Insight: If treats don't work, try toys or praise. A rigid trainer fails; a flexible one succeeds.

Leadership Lesson: In leadership, adaptability is crucial. Different situations and people require different approaches. Flexibility keeps growth possible.

Reflection: Where could I try a different approach instead of sticking rigidly to one way?

Anticipate Distractions

Dog Training Insight: A trainer knows the dog will bolt if a squirrel runs by, so they prepare.

Leadership Lesson: Leaders should anticipate challenges and distractions, planning ahead so teams don't get derailed.

Reflection: What potential challenges might derail my team this week, and how can I prepare?

Be Patient With Setbacks

Dog Training Insight: Even a well-trained dog sometimes forgets. Setbacks are part of learning.

Leadership Lesson: Employees may regress under stress or change. A setback isn't failure. It's a chance to reinforce lessons and keep moving forward.

Reflection: How do I typically react when progress backslides? What could I do differently?

Curiosity Beats Force

Dog Training Insight: A dog explores a new object more willingly if they can sniff and discover it at their own pace. Forcing it only creates fear.

Leadership Lesson: Employees adapt more quickly when invited to be curious instead of pressured. Encourage exploration rather than demanding compliance.

Reflection: How can I spark curiosity instead of pushing compliance?

Avoid Flooding the Senses

Dog Training Insight: Overwhelming a dog with too many sights and sounds during training leads to shutdown, not learning.

Leadership Lesson: Employees also shut down when overloaded with information or demands. Leaders should introduce change gradually and intentionally.

Reflection: Where might I be overwhelming my team with too much change or information?

Anticipate Growth Spurts

Dog Training Insight: A puppy who seems calm may suddenly test boundaries during adolescence, it's part of growing up.

Leadership Lesson: Employees also hit phases of rapid growth or testing limits. Leaders who anticipate this can respond with guidance instead of frustration.

Reflection: Who on my team might be ready for a leap forward, and how can I guide them?

Leadership Is About Patience

Dog Training Insight: The "in-between" stage when a dog knows the command but isn't reliable yet can be frustrating.

Leadership Lesson: Teams also go through messy middle stages where progress is uneven. Great leaders stay patient and keep reinforcing until reliability develops.

Reflection: What "messy middle" am I or my team currently in, and how can I show patience?

Energy Is Contagious

Dog Training Insight: A nervous handler creates a nervous dog. A calm presence reassures.

Leadership Lesson: Leaders set the emotional tone for their teams. Calm, confident leadership reduces stress, while frantic energy spreads just as quickly.

Reflection: What energy am I bringing into the room and is it what I want my team to mirror?

Leadership Happens Between Sessions

Dog Training Insight: Dogs don't just learn during training, they're always observing your behavior.

Leadership Lesson: Employees learn just as much from what you model outside of formal meetings as they do in structured settings. Leadership is lived in the everyday moments.

Reflection: What message am I sending my team in the "in-between" moments of the day?

Consistency Across Handlers

Dog Training Insight: A dog gets confused if one family member says "off" and another says "down." Mixed signals slow learning.

Leadership Lesson: Teams also struggle when leaders give conflicting instructions. Consistency across managers creates clarity, while mixed messages breed frustration.

Reflection: Where might my team be hearing mixed signals from me or other leaders and how can we align better?

Celebrate Progress, Not Just Perfection

Dog Training Insight: A crooked "sit" is still progress compared to no response at all.

Leadership Lesson: Perfection isn't the only marker of success. Leaders who recognize progress keep people motivated and learning.

Reflection: Where can I spotlight effort and growth, not just flawless results?

Listen as Much as You Talk

Dog Training Insight: Good trainers watch the dog's reaction before giving more direction.

Leadership Lesson: Leadership isn't only about telling, it's also about listening. Pay attention to feedback and response before moving forward.

Reflection: When was the last time I truly listened without planning my response?

Leadership Is a Relationship

Dog Training Insight: A dog follows because of the bond, not just the command.

Leadership Lesson: Employees commit when they trust the relationship. Leadership is less about authority and more about connection.

Reflection: How am I nurturing my relationship with my team beyond just tasks?

Trust Is Earned, Not Demanded

Dog Training Insight: You can't demand trust from a dog, you earn it by showing up consistently.

Leadership Lesson: Titles don't guarantee respect. Trust grows through actions, fairness, and reliability over time.

Reflection: What have I done lately to earn trust, not just expect it?

Balance Discipline With Affection

Dog Training Insight: A firm "no" has power when paired with plenty of praise and affection.

Leadership Lesson: Accountability works best when balanced with care. Employees need both correction and encouragement to thrive.

Reflection: Do my people know I care about them, even when I hold them accountable?

Rest Is Part of Training

Dog Training Insight: Dogs consolidate learning during downtime. Overwork diminishes progress.

Leadership Lesson: Rest and recovery fuel performance. Leaders who respect work-life balance build healthier, more effective teams.

Reflection: How am I modeling and encouraging rest for myself and my team?

Be Clear About Non-Negotiables

Dog Training Insight: Safety rules, like not running into the road, are non-negotiable. Dogs must learn them clearly.

Leadership Lesson: Leaders must identify and communicate the rules in their workplace, standards that are non-negotiable for safety, ethics, or values. Without clarity, people guess, and guessing leads to mistakes.

Reflection: *Have I clearly stated the values or standards that are non-negotiable in my workplace?*

Practice in Real Situations

Dog Training Insight: Practicing "heel" in the living room is different from walking past squirrels in the park. Real life is the true test.

Leadership Lesson: Skills need to be applied in real-world conditions, not just theory. Leaders should create opportunities for practice in authentic contexts where challenges actually happen.

Reflection: How can I create more opportunities for practice in real-world contexts?

Training Never Truly Ends

Dog Training Insight: Even an old dog still benefits from practice and refreshers. Learning is lifelong.

Leadership Lesson: Leadership development doesn't stop with a promotion or a title. The best leaders keep learning, growing, and practicing throughout their careers.

Reflection: What's one area of leadership I want to keep learning about this year?

Celebrate the Journey, Not Just the Goal

Dog Training Insight: Teaching agility is about enjoying the small breakthroughs along the way, not only winning ribbons.

Leadership Lesson: Leadership is about valuing progress, effort, and growth, not just final results. Teams stay motivated when the journey itself is honored, not just the destination.

Reflection: How can I pause to honor how far we've come, not just how far we have left to go?

Congratulations!

You've just spent an entire year investing in your leadership, one small lesson at a time. That's no small feat. Just as a well-trained dog doesn't happen overnight, neither does strong leadership. It's built through daily choices, weekly reflection, and consistent effort.

You've discovered that leadership is less about authority and more about relationships. You've seen how patience pays off, how consistency builds trust, and how encouragement changes behavior faster than criticism ever could. You've learned that leadership isn't about perfection—it's about progress, presence, and persistence.

And you've learned, the work is never really finished. There's always another opportunity to refine, to grow, and to learn something new about yourself and your team. The goal isn't to "arrive" at leadership, it's to keep becoming the kind of leader others want to follow.

So celebrate the journey. Celebrate the fact that you've paused each week to reflect, to learn, and to grow. Carry these lessons forward into the weeks and years to come. And when you do, the results are lasting and rewarding for both you and those you lead.

About the Author

Marty Pearson, PHR, SHRM-CP, is an executive coach, leadership trainer, and the founder of LFT Consulting, where she helps leaders create strong, healthy teams through clarity, communication, and consistency.

With over two decades of experience in Human Resources, organizational development, and leadership training, Marty has worked closely with executives, leadership teams, and HR professionals across diverse industries. Her work focuses on helping leaders move beyond theory and into practical, people-centered leadership that actually works in the real world.

While Marty's professional background is extensive, she's quick to say that some of her most meaningful leadership lessons came from outside traditional workplaces. Training her strong-willed dog, Beanie, became an unexpected masterclass in patience, clear communication, consistency, and self-awareness—skills that translate directly into effective leadership. Those everyday moments inspired the relatable stories and insights woven throughout her work.

Marty believes leadership is built one moment at a time. Her philosophy emphasizes progress over perfection, intentional reinforcement of desired behaviors, and the power of slowing down to lead with mindfulness, kindness, and confidence. Through executive coaching, workshops, and leadership development programs, she equips leaders to build trust, strengthen relationships, and create sustainable cultures where people can do their best work.

Outside of her professional life, Marty is a lifelong adventurer and learner. She's an avid traveler who has camped in the Serengeti with elephants and giraffes wandering nearby, and cruised Antarctic waters close enough to humpback whales and orcas to feel their presence. She's also a devoted coffee enthusiast, a black belt in Taekwondo, a former scuba diving instructor of ten years, and has completed 53 solo skydives—each experience reinforcing her belief that growth happens just beyond our comfort zone.

When she's not coaching leaders or exploring the world, Marty continues learning leadership lessons alongside her dog—one week at a time.

Work with Marty

Listen to our Podcast: Build A Better Business on
Apple, Spotify, or wherever you
get your podcasts.

LFT Consulting

Lead with Confidence
Focus on Your People
Transform Your Business

www.lftconsult.com

www.ingramcontent.com/pod-product-compliance
Lightning Source LLC
Chambersburg PA
CBHW041144120626
46547CB00020B/3095